Add a Little Colour to your Life

Mark Wentworth

CONTENTS

ACKNOWLEDGEMENTS 1

INTRODUCTION 3

COLOUR ANALYSIS 9

THE POWER OF COLOUR IN CLOTHING 14

COLOUR HEALING 20

LIFE PATH COLOURS..30

    Life Path Colour – RED 35

    Life Path Colour – ORANGE...................................37

    Life Path Colour – YELLOW 39

    Life Path Colour – GREEN 41

    Life Path Colour – BLUE.......................................43

    Life Path Colour – INDIGO 45

    Life Path Colour – VIOLET...................................47

    Life Path Colour – ROSE 50

    Life Path Colour – GOLD 52

ACKNOWLEDGEMENTS

This small booklet is just the beginning...

It is dedicated to two very special people.

To Linda, for all the fun, laughter, love and tears, and long may the journey continue.

To William, you came into my life just when I needed you most. You brought light where there had been darkness.

Special thanks to the people who have believed and supported me in my work, both past and present.

An especially big thank you to the few whom found it difficult to believe, for it was you that helped me persevere.

INTRODUCTION

Welcome to the wonderful world of colour. Colour is something, which is there and always will be there. It is something that I believe we take for granted; hopefully by the end of this booklet you will share a similar view to my own. Colour is a wonderful gift, when we begin to understand the power of colour; we begin to see how everyone and everything is inter-linked. By developing colour consciousness, we develop self-awareness; having self-awareness we have forgiveness and understanding. By having all of these, we have most importantly love, self-love, love of others and love of everything created in the universe.

Let there be Colour

Let there be Life

Mother Nature has provided us with all the necessary tools and ingredients to heal ourselves. They are all there, all we need to do is take time to look – we have herbs, we have essential oils from flowers and plants, and most importantly we have colour.

Colour is around us every day of our lives; research is showing that we are affected by colour even before birth. It is often the things that are right in front of us, that have the most healing effect.

Colour is made from refracted light, I'm sure we all remember our physics lessons, playing with prisms, colour filters and learning the make up of certain colours.

White is not considered to be a colour because it contains all colours. Black is also not regarded as a colour because it absorbs all light and therefore cannot reflect back colour.

Everything in the universe has a rate of oscillation, every tree, and every plant, bird, animal, and right down to the smallest atom.

Rocks, metals and man-made fibres, all vibrate at a certain rate, the slower the rate of vibration, the more dense the material, thus as we see it, the less of a living thing it is. When you start to realise this, you realise that everything and everyone is interconnected. Each colour has a specific rate of vibration, red being the slowest and violet being the fastest. It is proven that the faster the rate of vibration the further from physical life one becomes hence the reason Violet is often used in spiritual practices and pursuits. Also people who have 'near death' experiences talk of seeing a great white light – white contains all colours, therefore can be seen to contain all aspects of spiritual life. In the Bible, God says 'Let there be light' after light came physical life – the slowing down of vibration to form physical life.

Each colour creates a different emotional and psychological reaction; advertisers and the media often use it, to help promote a certain idea, or sell a particular product. One of the more obvious examples of colour in action is to look at the use of **Red**. **Red** commands attention, it calls for us to act immediately – red road signs, red traffic lights and a red flag at the beach, all convey a similar message, STOP AND TAKE NOTICE.

Red is commonly used when a shop has a sale; if you look around, you will see red is used in fairly large amounts. We react immediately, we buy impulsively, tempers may flare (as someone tries to get the same item you've seen) but the message is still the same... BUY NOW! Not tomorrow or next week but do it NOW!

Red is also used in fast food restaurants - that is because red stimulates the appetite and it does not encourage you to stay for too long. You can begin to see how red is used on a subtle level to get the message across.

All colours work on a subtle level, so it is very important to consider the colours you choose when decorating. You can create any mood or atmosphere by adding particular colours to an environment. Consider the main activity taking place within that environment, and then decorate accordingly.

Listed below are some guidelines to using different colours for décor: -

RED – This is probably better used as 'splashes of ' rather than en mass, as red can be confrontational, and in most cases, too demanding. The results of red are short lived. It may be a quick booster of energy but the energy will decrease just as fast. Use dark reds to give a feeling of richness and opulence.

ORANGE – This includes peach/apricot. Orange is good for promoting self-esteem and nurturing the inner-child. In décor it wraps you up in your own security and makes you feel safe. Orange is made up from an equal mix of red and yellow, however, peach has more red and apricot has more yellow. Therefore, apricot is good in boardrooms or other such rooms used for debates, as yellow stimulates the thinking process. Peach is good for anchoring emotionally charged situations and helps to promote individuality.

YELLOW – Yellow stimulates the left side of the brain. It's good for promoting logical thinking. Yellow is an excellent colour for studies as it helps you to absorb more information. It also stimulates the short-term memory. Yellow is not a good colour for bedrooms or any other relaxation areas, physically you would relax but your mind would remain alert and eventually would lead to mental agitation.

GREEN – This colour gives structure and boundaries to the environment. Green is the colour of replenishment and nature, it promotes movement and change but in a secure and structured manner. This is a good colour to decorate rooms where you have 'time out'; it gives you space and time to rebalance.

BLUE – Relaxation, peace and daydreams are all the things you feel when in a room decorated in blue. It lifts you away from your physical surroundings and helps you to de-stress. Blue is often used in pre-op wards in hospitals and sometimes in dentist's waiting rooms. Blue is most commonly known as a healing colour, it promotes the feeling of 'being cared for'; which is why traditionally a nurse's uniform is blue.

INDIGO – Indigo is deep and enticing, it is scary to some and yet a welcome escape for others. Indigo, like blue, invites you to pause and take a deep breath; it opens a door into other worlds. It's a great colour for a bedroom, although for some it can be too intense. Use Indigo if you have difficulty in dreaming or you want to deepen your dream experiences. If you want to add a touch of mystery and magic to any room Indigo will be happy to oblige.

VIOLET/PURPLE – These are colours to be used in rooms for deep relaxation and meditation, or any environment you want to have an 'out of this world feeling'. As with red this colour is better used as 'splashes of ' rather than a main colour, this is because long term effects can be depressive and give a feeling of dizziness and not being grounded. Violet/purple promote creativity and stimulate the right side of the brain.

PINK – From the palest innocence of baby pink, the unconditional love of rose pink, right through to the passion of Magenta and Fuchsia, pink is the colour we most associate with love. The softer pinks are great to use in a room where you need to get to the "heart of the problem" it offers unconditional support. A slightly deeper pink has been used in prisons and police stations to calm aggression; in pink it's just not possible to be aggressive. Used in a bedroom Rose is soothing and adds a heart-warming glow to the room.

GOLD – Gold can fill you with warmth and bring a smile to your face, it offers hope for the future and helps heal wounds of the past. Imagine a room decorated with the gold's of sunrise or sunset and your room will be filled with that same hope and optimism. Gold soothes the nerves and replenishes the Soul. The metallic golds add a touch of class and opulence to any space they fall upon.

BLACK – A dark mood or dramatically beautiful, both describe the colour black. It is a colour of extremes, it is used to hide something and yet it can also enhance whatever comes near it. In décor it offers contrast and makes the colours surrounding it that little bit more intense. Similar to the metallic golds it too can bring a touch of class to a room.

WHITE – As cold as snow or as warm as the heart of divinity and like its black counterpart, white is a colour of extremes. Use it in décor to create space, freshness and a place to just be.

Always remember to consider the main activity of the environment and start from there, if an area has more than one use, consider using moveable items which can be added or removed as required. For example, if you have a relaxation area but also want to use it as a study area, introduce something yellow, i.e. a lamp or even simpler, a piece of yellow fabric or paper placed under the study material will have the same effect. Remember that we not only absorb colour through vision but we absorb colour through the skin, therefore colour affects everyone. It makes no difference if a person has no sight or is colour blind, they are still affected by colour, and colour works on the whole person and is available to all.

COLOUR ANALYSIS

Colour in clothing is using this wonderful gift from nature to help promote us as balanced and harmonious human beings, whoever we may be.

Colour analysis is the art of finding colours which best reflect us as individuals, enabling us to feel and look confident about who we are. By wearing the colours, which suit our natural hair colour, eye colour, and skin tone, we create a feeling of self-worth and project the image of wholeness. The idea is that when you walk into a room people notice all of you and not just your clothing or in the case of a woman, her make-up. We all have an undertone to our skin colouring that is either cool or warm. We need to wear colours that harmonise with our own personal colouring.

Listed are some of the characteristics to help you determine which of the four seasons you belong to.

Look at the palms of the hands, for a cool person the palms will appear to have a slight blue/pink colouring, for a warm person the palms will appear to have an orange/yellow tone. Colouring beneath the eye can also indicate a person's skin tone, a purple or bluish cast again indicate a cool tone, if these areas have a golden colouring this person most definitely belongs to the warm tone selection. Continuing the link with nature, the warm undertones are divided into two of the four seasons, which are Autumn and Spring, the cool tones relate to Summer and Winter. If you really cannot decide which season a person belongs to, ask which colours they are drawn to, interestingly most people instinctively choose colours from their own season.

Listed are eye, hair and skin colourings for each of the seasons.

Warm seasons have a yellow tone to the colours and possibly the best example of this, is looking at a warm red. Look at the red fabric and you will see it has, although red, a slight yellow tinge.

AUTUMN

Eyes – Light golden brown, pale clear green, hazel, golden green or turquoise.

Hair – Brown, chestnut, copper, auburn, red, light golden brown, dark golden blonde.

Skin – Dark brown, golden brown, peach, golden beige, creamy white.

Clothing – Rich warm colours, green, rust, terracotta, khaki, gold, forest green, olive, orange, turquoise, teal, tomato red, oyster white, chocolate brown.

Autumn types are earthy, independent characters; they are also warm and friendly.

SPRING

Eyes – Blue with yellow flecks, golden green, light golden brown, amber, turquoise, grey.

Hair – Flaxen blonde, golden blonde, strawberry blonde, light golden blonde.

Skin – Peach, light cream, ivory, freckle.

Clothing – Clear warm colours – Ivory white, camel, coral, lime green, periwinkle blue, orange – reds, warm violet, apricot, peach.

Spring types are lively, vivacious and can have a tendency to be disorganised. They are always full of new ideas and life. Think of the season!

Cool seasons have a blue tone to the colours, and again the best example of this is to look at a cool red. You will see, although red, it has a blue tinge to its colouring.

WINTER

Eyes – Blue with white flecks, dark brown, hazel, grey rim around the iris.

Hair – Black, dark brown, mid brown, silver grey, white.

Skin – Rose beige, olive brown, black.

Clothing – Clear bright colours – magenta, black, white, royal blue, royal purple, emerald green, blue reds.

Winter types are dramatic, like the season, they can appear confident but are often quite shy.

SUMMER

Eyes – Blue with white flecks, hazel/blue brown, grey blue, clear blue, grey rim around iris.

Hair – Platinum, ash blonde, mousy, light to medium brown.

Skin – Pink beige, pale pink cheeks, pale beige.

Clothing – Soft cool colours – soft white, rose beige, rose red, light blue red, medium blue, light silver grey, light navy, lilac.

Summer types are warm, loving and reserved.

There are apparently more winter types in the world than any other season.

Even when you belong to a particular season, you will probably not suit every colour from that palette, choose colours which reflect how you feel at that particular time. When we choose colours to wear, it is the subconscious, which selects the colours; the choice will be the colours that mirror our deepest feelings. The colours will best support our emotional state at that moment in time, which is why, one day you will feel and look good in a certain colour and yet another time you will not feel so confident with the colour. This can explain why, when you try an item of clothing on in a shop, especially if the shop has many red sale signs, the clothing looks fantastic. Try on the same item of clothing a few hours later and somehow it doesn't look or feel quite the same, if you were to check your emotional state, you would

find it would have been different to when you first
bought the item.

THE POWER OF COLOUR IN CLOTHING

If you take a look in your wardrobe there's probably quite a lot of your favourite colours in here. The colours you choose to wear are possibly your greatest expression of who you are and how bold you dare to go with experimenting with colour. But wait, what about those items of clothing you did buy but haven't quite got round to wearing yet? It's not so much about the item of clothing but more about the colour of it. These hidden colours could be likened to seeds that are waiting to germinate and bring new adventures into your life. The list below can help you translate what those "seeds" maybe trying to tell you.

When reading the list of colours and their meanings do keep in mind that each colour has many shades and tones. The important thing is to find the right one for you. If you decide, for example, that you want some Pink, find the right shade of pink that you feel comfortable with. If you are unsure which tone of a colour you need, refer back to the section on Colour Analysis and use what you think is your seasonal palette as a starting point.

By consciously choosing the colours you wear, you then have the possibility create the right impression and image that you want to create.

RED

Wear red to: - command attention, attract a partner (too much red would make the experience short-lived!), convey strength of character, when you want to win.

Avoid red when: - overtired, and when you are not sure of the situation, it can make others confrontational.

ORANGE

Wear orange: - to boost self-worth, to have fun and self-indulge, without feeling guilty. Orange/peach are colours to wear if you work as a counsellor or social worker. Wearing these colours will also help you to understand the roots and meaning of sociology.

Avoid orange: - when attending interviews, it tends to unnerve the interviewer. This colour stimulates our need and want for sweeter tasting foods. There is little self-control with orange.

YELLOW

Wear yellow when: - You need to have fun and bring some joy into your life. Wear pale yellow when working or playing with young children. Wear yellow when you need to focus and pay attention to detail.

Avoid yellow: - If over-stressed and you can only see the worm's eye view of a situation. Avoid black and bright yellow, the message it gives is the same as the one in nature, "don't come to close, there's a nasty sting in my tail!"

GREEN

Wear green: - when you want personal space, when over-stressed, when you need a balanced level headed approach. True green and light green offer freshness and restoration.

Avoid dark green if trying to promote new ideas, this colour does not offer change. However, it is a good colour if working in financial areas.

BLUE

Navy projects authority, honesty, and trust (the colour of police/security uniforms)

Mid-blue – the colour for interviews, it inspires open communication and helps the wearer remain cool and calm.

Light blue – when caring for others. (Avoid this colour if you do not want to hear everyone else's problems)

INDIGO

Wear it in its truest form as an alternative to black to create an air of mystery, it commands respect and in its own way demands to be noticed. Wear Indigo if you want to evoke intuition both in yourself and in others.

Avoid wearing Indigo if you have a tendency to daydream, it will only make you dream further.

PURPLE

Wear purple: - to project confidence and individuality, and as another alternative to black. The Violet aspect of purple inspires creativity, and right brain activity.

Avoid Purple: - when dealing with mental illness and when you yourself feel depressed, as this colour has the potential to exacerbate the feelings.

PINK

Wear pink to: - Promote the teamwork approach; it evokes compassion and is a great colour for creating romance.

Avoid pink when: - you want to be number one, discussing promotion, when you want to remain level headed (too much pink can give you the rose tinted glasses syndrome).

WHITE

Wear white for freshness and its purity has a youthful appeal to it too. It promotes the sense of capability and being both approachable and untouchable at the same time.

Avoid white: Can also give the feeling of being cold and detached emotionally.

GREY

Light grey reflects whatever you wear with it; it acts like an artist's canvas. It also helps the wearer to remain emotionally neutral.

Dark grey conveys the message of strict boundaries and rules (perhaps the reason why, this colour is used a lot in school uniforms)

Grey is not a good colour to wear when working with young children, as it offers no emotional support.

BLACK

Wear black: - to create impact, to hide behind and remain mysterious.

Avoid black: - when you or others around you feel depressed. When you have to be open and honest, (the colour creates a contradiction).

Remember that the colour of the clothes you wear will not only affect you, but they will influence the people around you. Research shows that we respond to 93% non-verbal communication, 55% of that is from body language, part of which includes visual appearance. In a split second, based in part on how the person looks and the colours they are wearing we have already decided as to how we will react to this person.

So the colours we wear play a big part in non-verbal communication. If you wear something Red, for example, you can expect to be challenged on what you say or do, Red conveys confidence and strength of character, so you need to feel that confidence in order to be it. As a colour it also can evoke competitiveness, which is why some people feel wary of including Red in their wardrobe.

Many people have often asked why teenagers are drawn towards wearing black; my own theory on this is as follows. Firstly, we must remember that black absorbs all light and colour, but if you think of planting a seed in the ground, in effect you are planting that seed in blackness. Yet the seed germinates, grows roots and eventually a shoot appears above the surface. Now, consider what happens during teenage years, adolescence, puberty, and body and hormonal changes all changes below the surface. They question who they are, and what they want in life, all is somewhat similar to the seed beneath the soil. After a time, you start to see traces of colour emerging once more into their lives.

Many people are drawn to wear black or dark shades of colour when they are going through deep emotional changes, it offers the feeling of safety and security, until they are ready to emerge and show to the world this new found element.

COLOUR HEALING

The colours we choose to surround ourselves with, be it décor or clothing, is all part of the subconscious communicating where we are on the journey of life.

People's dislike of certain colours can often reveal unresolved emotional issues; colour is just the key to unlocking the door of deep-seated and often painful memories. Dislike of colour, has nothing really to do with the colour, it is more to do with the association, i.e. think of all the people who refuse to wear a certain colour, whatever their age, because it immediately reminds them of school uniform. When we have a traumatic experience, we often block out the trauma as way of self-protection. The subconscious will choose a key to represent the experience, and that key happens to be colour. In addition, if we are not expressing our true potential, again the subconscious will reflect this with colour.

E.G., A client had a strong dislike of pink. Seeing the colour would bring tears and a great feeling of loss. On further exploration, she remembered that as a child she had witnessed her dog being hit by a car, at the time of the incident she was standing by a newly painted pink door.

Another client found purple most uncomfortable, her body language would become closed and her breathing quite shallow, the colour to her was cold and harsh. She would describe herself as having no creative talent and no belief in any kind of religion. As a young child, she had been sent to a convent boarding school, which she found to be cold and harsh. Before going to this school, she showed a slant towards creativity. During a consultation, the fact suddenly came to light, that her school uniform had been predominantly purple. Following this realisation, she was able to integrate purple back into her life, and rediscover latent talents that had been frozen in time due to these associations. Later she found affinity with the spiritualist movement and today works as a spiritual healer.

The aim of colour therapy is to treat the cause and not the symptom; colour is a supportive, non-invasive way of helping people to deal with difficult situations. The idea is to desensitise people to colour, so they are then able to bring the whole visible spectrum into their world and live totally in the light.

Each part of the body relates to a different colour (Diagram 1), there are seven main colours to work with. They are Red, Orange, Yellow, Green, Blue, Indigo, and Violet. The body is made up of a map of energy points; and this map helps guide acupuncturists, for example, to know where to place the needles. Within this map are seven major energy points running the length of the spine, from the bottom of the spine, right to the top of the head. Each of these major points relates to one of the seven colours. (Diagram 1) The energy points have an ancient Sanskrit name, which is Chakra, translated this means, spinning vortex of energy.

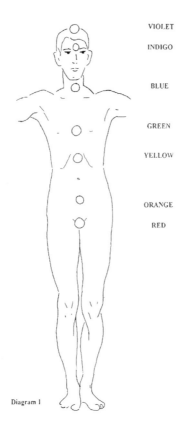

VIOLET

INDIGO

BLUE

GREEN

YELLOW

ORANGE

RED

Diagram 1

All chakras are interlinked and each has its own physical, psychological, emotional, mental, and spiritual associations and functions, right down to even being connected with different chronological and developmental stages of life.

The chakra points relate to: -

BASE.... RED.... 0 – 2 Years.

SACRAL.... ORANGE.... 2 – 4 Years.

SOLAR.... YELLOW.... 4 – End of education.

HEART.... GREEN.... Building a life for oneself.

THROAT.... BLUE.... To know and understand why we act the way we do.

BROW.... INDIGO.... To enjoy rewards from building life.

CROWN.... VIOLET.... To fulfill our greatest potential.

Psychologist, Abraham Maslow, came up with the theory that human needs, such as intellectual needs, esteem needs, all form a hierarchy. In order for healthy individual development each need has to be fulfilled before one can move onto the next level (See diagram 2).

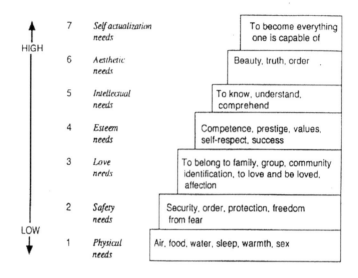

Diagram 2

Interestingly I noticed a correlation between each chakra point and Maslow's hierarchical needs. For example, the base chakra relates to the ages of birth to two years which, if you consider the most important needs of a child of this age, it will be physical needs, air, food, water, sleep and warmth, these needs are first in Maslow's hierarchy.

The **Base chakra** is responsible for rooting us to the earth and helping us to function in the here and now. If someone has experienced some kind of trauma at this stage of life, the base will not have developed properly, thus causing dysfunction and problems later in adult life. How this might manifest, would be the inability to settle in one place for too long, constantly being uprooted or withholding anger, which could eventually translate into bone problems or hot skin complaints. In personal relationships this person can become domineering or take the passive role, if they decide on this role, the other person is always seen as much more powerful.

Expressed base energy is spontaneous and gives power to your hopes and aspirations. Base energy gives the spark to life and the ability to live life to the full. Male libido is proposed by some theories, to be held in this centre, which could go to explain why, for some men, sex is mostly to do with the physical act. Women on the other hand, it is proposed, hold their libido in the next chakra which primarily governs the emotions, which again could explain why, for a lot of women, sex has much more of an emotional component to it.

The **Sacral chakra** nourishes us and helps to feel good emotionally about who we are. Through this centre we experience how we relate to the world around us and how the world relates to us.

If we feel fear and unsafe emotionally we learn early on not to rely on others, and either develop strong walls or keep the walls down constantly hoping someone will meet our early unmet emotional needs. When the Sacral Chakra is wounded we either become a master at people pleasing or totally detached and relating to no one. Abdominal issues, lower back pain and gynaecological problems for women are expressions of an unhappy sacral chakra.

Healthy sacral energy is fun loving, and allows us to enjoy the pleasures of all that life has to offer and fully experiencing every single minute of it.

The **Solar Plexus chakra** strengthens our sense of identity and character and when we know who we are, we know where we belong and which groups support our identity and which don't. If we learn that who we are is not ok we quickly adapt to fit in and in so doing the grey skies come and our true light never shines through. We either become depressed with no hope or become super efficient and hyper attentive to make sure we always fit in and do the right thing. Stomach, liver, kidney and bladder issues tell us when the sun is overshadowed for the solar plexus.

When the solar plexus shines the whole world feels lighter and brighter. We find the right people to fit in our circle, we feel supported to let our true-self shine through. Life is good, life is happy.

The **Heart Chakra** reminds us that there is love in the world and if we have love we can pretty much do anything. The heart chakra gives us our core values and when we know these we can build and create healthy boundaries for ourselves and those we love. When boundaries get broken and love is betrayed the heart chakra shrinks back and is replaced with the sharp thorns of jealousy and bitterness, what was once beautiful becomes gnarled and withered. Physical problems related to the mid back, shoulders, arms and hands, along with the lungs and the heart reminds us that love doesn't live here anymore.

The loving heart loves and is loved, not just for another, but also for all things that exist. We feel inspired to create home both as a physical space and a place within. The heart chakra teaches us that wherever we are, we are always connected and always home.

The **Throat chakra** helps us to express our truth and gives us the ability to listen in order to comprehend others. We speak what inspires us and share what comes from both the heart and the heavens. When our truth is shouted down we learn to be silent and not ask for what we want, instead we learn to eat our truth and swallow it down with food and drink. When our voice becomes silent so to do our ears and the nose suffers too. Ear, nose and throat issues remind us that our voice needs to be heard.

When the throat chakra is clear we know the song in our heart and teach those close to us what is so that if we forget they can sing it back to us. From the throat chakra we speak our truth and through our truth comes our healing.

The **Brow chakra** invites us to dream and see with a hundred eyes. Through the brow chakra we can see out beyond the invisible and in through the darkness. Colours and patterns that you will never see are as clear as the light of day, look with logic and a closed mind and nothing will you see. When our ideas are consistently analysed and criticised our dreams turn colourless and drudgery and mundane become the norm. Eye problems, sinus issues, headaches and migraines all tell us that we need to dream again.

The brow chakra helps us to imagine the life we could live; it brings the clues and shows us the treasure map of our life purpose. It helps us to see clearly on all levels of being.

The **Crown Chakra** connects us to all that is, it links us with all that we believe to be God, Goddess, Universe, whatever our belief, the crown chakra connects us to it and to all those who share our same belief. It is the connector of the Collective. Harm comes when we are told what and whom we should believe without being able to decide for ourselves. Harm comes when our way decides that another belief is wrong and should be suppressed, damage comes when we dehumanise another for the sake of the collective belief. Headaches, the inability to think clearly for ourselves, and nerve conditions are all messengers that ask us if we are truly connected with our higher divinity.

The crown chakra in all its magnificence inspires us to be all that we were born to be, we know without question that we are guided and supported both from within and from beyond. And in our becoming we inspire others to follow their own path.

Balancing Chakras

To help balance a chakra you can either meditate with the colour associated with it, or you can wear the colour you need to balance, or even simply place a coloured piece of material over the part of the body relating to the chakra. These seemingly simple actions will help to re-balance and recharge the chakra in question. Try it and see, I think you will be quite surprised as to what happens and how you feel. When we act, colour responds.

LIFE PATH COLOURS

Finding your life path colour is an ancient art, which turns your date of birth into one of nine colours. Discovering your life path colour helps you to know and understand why you do the things you do, and why you react to situations in a particular way. It can also reveal what kind of career you would be best suited to e.g. as a yellow person, you could easily work with figures, be a scientist, or market researcher. As an orange person, a counsellor, politician or union representative. A life path colour indicates in which part of the body stress is most likely to manifest, and how best to deal with it. Because all colours create an emotional reaction, knowing your own colour shows how you will relate to others on an emotional level.

Adding all the numbers in your birth date together and then reducing them to a single number between-1 – 9 derives a life path colour.

i.e. 16.3.1969

$$1 + 6 + 3 + 1 + 9 + 6 + 9 = 35 = 3 + 5 = 8$$

The numbers must always be reduced to a single digit, do not forget to include the 19 in the year, no abbreviations i.e. 16.3.69.

Each of the single numbers relate to a particular colour which are as follows:

1 – Red

2 – Orange

3 – Yellow

4 – Green

5 – Blue

6 – Indigo

7 – Violet

8 – Rose

9 – Gold

It would be too much of an over-generalisation to divide the whole population into just nine colours. To make a life path colour more personal to the individual, we look at all the names the person has used since birth and turn those into colour. Each letter of the alphabet is associated with a number and as you remember, each number relates to a colour.

$$1 = A \; J \; S$$

$$2 = B \; K \; T$$

$$3 = C \; L \; U$$

$$4 = D \; M \; V$$

$$5 = E \; N \; W$$

$$6 = F \ O \ X$$

$$7 = G \ P \ Y$$

$$8 = H \ Q \ Z$$

$$9 = I \ R$$

So: A J S = 1 = Red

You can look at all or just one of your names, turn each letter into a number; add together until you come out with a single digit. By comparing the colours in your name to your life path, you get to see how you relate to your most fundamental personality traits. If you find you do not recognise certain characteristics within yourself, you will find the universe has a wonderful way of still bringing those parts into your life. The way this happens is you attract a partner, who exhibits the very characteristics you do not recognise in yourself, this goes part way to explain the powers of attraction.

If you find life is not working for you, introduce your life path colour into your environment and this will help re-align you with the journey you have chosen to make. Adding the colour to your life will give enlightenment and bring to the fore latent gifts and talents. Colour is a refraction of light, and light is essential for life itself to exist, therefore your life path colour is the key to the soul and all of its hidden treasures.

An easy way to understand how your name colour relates to your life path colour is to have either pieces of material, paper or paint of your two colours. Place your name colour on top of your life path colour, what does it look like? Do they compliment one another, or do they shout at each other, and seeing these two colours together, how do you feel, what images, thoughts do these colours bring up for you?

Following is an example of the whole process in action: -

$1 - 6 - 1926 = 1 + 6 + 1 + 9 + 2 + 6 = 25 = 2 + 5 = 7$

$7 = \text{Violet}$

Violet Life Path: -

One of a kind, could be compared to a delicate flower, incredibly sensitive, can have a tendency to escape into fantasy world. Often feels totally alone and different although surrounded by close friends.

NORMA JEANE BAKER

$5 \, 6 \, 9 \, 4 \, 1 \quad 151 \, 5 \, 5 \quad 2 \, 1 \, 2 \, 5 \, 9 = 61 = 6 + 1 = 7 - \text{Violet}$

Shows a sensitive child who would have created her own world of fantasy from an early age, mainly as a way of dealing with difficult outside influences, as such a form of self-protection. Also indicates an appreciation of beauty and wanting to surround oneself with such. Not surprisingly violet also governs the film industry and other such creative pursuits. Mother is shown to be more evident than father is, yet shows lack of emotional understanding of the sensitive child.

We now look at what happened to the child when she became known by a totally different name.

MARILYN MONROE

4 1 9 9 3 7 5   4 6 5 9 6 5 = 73 = 7 + 3 = 10 = 1 + 0 = 1 – Red

This shows a completely different person, a complete transformation. Red is a very physical colour and a magnetic colour, it draws attention to itself and demands to be noticed. Being the first colour in the spectrum, it could be looked upon as being quite childlike in its approach, giving an innocent appeal to this person's nature. Red also indicates a constant change of environment including the people within it.

The name Marilyn Monroe, suggests an attempt to escape from the delicate and sensitive Norma Jeane Baker, though somehow fits perfectly with the lessons and expectations of a violet life path, to leave their mark on the world and leave it a better place, than they originally found it.

Interestingly, both Diana Princess of Wales and Gianni Versace were on Violet life paths. Like Marilyn Monroe, both touched the world with their presence and helped the world become a more beautiful place.

Think of your life path colour much like the basic structure and foundations of a house. The colour within each name as the bricks and mortar, all help to build the house called "YOU".

Life Path Colour – RED

Active, dynamic, impulsive are but a few words to describe a Red life path. You live for the now, and want to experience everything for experience sake. Patience is a word, which does not exist in your vocabulary, and you expect everyone around you to be the same.

Red is the colour of action and you certainly know what you want and how you will get it. You could be your own boss any day, and if you are an employee, you prefer an easygoing boss and will probably be the one leading the rest. You speak your mind and say what you feel, sometimes leaving others shocked and open mouthed at your honesty and bluntness.

Being on a Red life path, you could easily be seen wearing bright colours and flamboyant clothing, something really to compliment your strong personality. People you surround yourself with are outgoing and energetic like yourself, and you would all be found at the leisure centre or at some other outdoor pursuit. You like to be constantly on the go and here I would draw your attention to the health aspects of a red life path. Take time to relax and recharge the batteries, otherwise you can suffer 'burn-out' and then you will feel frustration because you are physically not able to do the things you love to do. Be-aware of attracting heated situations into your life, or having minor knocks and bruises, this could indicate you are not being a true red life path – say what you are thinking!

Emotionally, you experience each emotion as though you have never experienced it before; you can be in-love, out of love, angry, sad, hurt, and frustrated, all in a short space of time. It is no use telling you how you were yesterday, that was then, this is now.

Red people are the pioneers of the spectrum, and want to be number One in everything they set out to do.

All in all this is a very urgent, excitable life path.

Life Path Colour – ORANGE

The fun loving energy that comes from the person on an Orange life path makes you a joy to be around. Your carefree, happy-go-lucky nature makes you a popular person to invite to any social gathering. Surprisingly enough show business and the entertainment industry comes under the influence of orange.

Food also plays an important part in your life, and could easily make a favourite hobby or indeed a good choice in a career move. Be-aware of not letting food become an emotional prop, either in overeating or not eating at all.

You are good at playing the mediator in any argument or debate, when asked for your own opinion, will pull out positive attributes from both sides. You believe everyone has the right to be who he or she wants to be, as long as it harms no one else. You will often advocate for a person or group if you feel they are getting a raw deal. Counselling, social work appeals, mainly because people turn to you for advice and a shoulder to cry on. Be careful not to take on other people's problems, learn to say 'NO'.

If your emotions seem to have ebbs and flows – check to see how they follow the moon's cycle, orange relates to the element of water. You could find you are very in-tune with that particular cycle. Then you can make plans for the best time to accomplish certain tasks, which need you to keep your emotions in check.

A patient, jovial and balanced life path.

Life Path Colour – YELLOW

Happy, cheerful and sunny describes someone on a Yellow life path. You give hope and optimism to others when they are feeling slightly off colour. You love socialising and people love to hear the stories that you tell, for you always have a way of spicing them up a bit, with your expansive imagination. Be careful of not letting your imagination run riot or starting too many things at once, so you end up "Jack of all trades- Master of none".

You have a fine mental intellect and we would find you surrounded by lots of books on many different subjects, or signing up for further education classes. You find people fascinating as long as they keep you interested, otherwise you can become bored relatively easily and it becomes obvious to those around, either by what you say or your expression.

You are able to analyse and pull out different pieces of information and to be honest – you truly would make a first rate private investigator!

With an eye for precise detail and an analytical mind, you will do well in banking, computers, marketing, or indeed a scientist. Because of your logical approach I am sure you would have understood Mr Spock from 'Star Trek' – an extreme example of a Yellow life path. In your mind, everything and everyone has their own little box, including emotions. There always has to be a logical reason for feeling.

In clothing, you prefer clear-cut, geometric style patterns, with borders and in bright colours. Your taste in music tends to be more classical and would enjoy such styles as Baroque.

Health problems such as nerves and mental stress seem to manifest themselves, first off in the stomach area. Insomnia can also cause problems. Try not to over-indulge with such things as caffeine, chocolate, or sugar, which all stimulate the mind and yours really is active enough.

People on Yellow life paths are stimulating, intelligent people to be with.

Life Path Colour – GREEN

You like having people around you as long as they do not crowd your space; you must be able to escape to a separate room or out into the garden if needs must. Your home is important to you and you will always strive to maintain a balanced harmonious environment. In décor you will chose pale tints of colour or surround yourself with natural woods, or houseplants, you like to be able to bring the outside, inside.

On a Green life path gives you natural affinity with nature, and when problems arise, you would best go to the countryside to think things through. Mother Nature, follows a specific pattern, we know that after winter, comes spring, after spring, follows summer and so on.

Similar to mother nature, Green people like to follow a set order, and often change can be difficult for you. You are accused of being stubborn and slow; it is more that you have to get used to the idea. You enjoy seeing tasks through to the very end, no matter how mundane or uninteresting, even when the going gets tough and others have given up long ago, you will hang on in to see the job finished. Be-aware of not holding on to old emotional baggage, if you find this happening, it is time to spring clean the cupboards, not only in a physical sense, but mentally and emotionally.

You are very practical in all that you do, and have flair for creating harmony where there has previously been disharmony. A balanced lifestyle is your ideal, if for some reason life becomes unbalanced, it affects you deeply and your natural instinct is to restore equilibrium at whatever cost.

At times of stress, you feel as though you are tied up in knots and the more you push, the more trapped you feel.

Remember limitations and restrictions are all of our own making, work within the boundaries and life feels less restrictive. Life is much like an ever-expanding spiral, no beginning and no end, the only thing we can guarantee, is change.

Stress manifests as tension in the shoulders, mid-back, also as breathing problems, such as asthma, bronchitis, and other chest related conditions.

Life Path Colour – BLUE

A Blue life path is one of tranquility, daydreams, and peace.

A Blue life path makes you a natural healer; a career in the medical profession either as a doctor or nurse would appeal, as would a career involving lots of communication. You need to be able to communicate and say all you need to, otherwise throat problems will occur, be it a sore throat, irritating cough, or tonsillitis all indicate there is something on your mind, which you are not saying.

Trust and honesty are necessary, this is what you give and this is what you expect in return, there can be no grey areas as far as those are concerned. Children recognise this and will be drawn to you, for not only do you care, but also you can relate to their world of make-believe.

You really would make a wonderful storyteller, be-aware of not letting this spill over into everyday life.

Music and sound are prominent in your life; most importantly, it has to be the right piece of music at the correct pitch, otherwise your whole system becomes irritated, and it is one of the easiest ways for you to feel stressed. Maybe you sing in a choir, play a musical instrument, or just have an ear for music. Music with a slight religious connection appeals, maybe something such as chant or choral. Keeping with the religious theme, you will find churches or other places of worship; give you a feeling of peace and tranquility.

Daydreams have been part of your life for as way back as you can remember, this enables you to turn ideas into realities.

Following on with the theme of daydreams, how many times have you been told to stop living in the clouds and keep your feet on the ground? This is also your way of dealing with difficult situations, withdrawing and saying nothing, which obviously in turn leads to throat problems.

This is a caring, creative life path – enjoy all it has to offer.

Life Path Colour – INDIGO

You are perceptive and have the ability to see how and why people act the way, they do.

Indigo lays between blue and violet in the colour spectrum. It is often a colour, which is not truly recognised, to some it will always remain a mystery. This is how you appear to others, outwardly you could be regarded as stable and sound, even if underneath there is lots going on for you. People turn to you for advice, because you have the ability to see the bird's eye view instead of the worm's eye position! People ask for your support, but do not forget that it works both ways, and it's OK to turn to others when you are in need.

Psychic ability is prominent; you have a kind of sixth sense. At times you may feel fearful of this gift, allow it to develop and you will find it will never let you down. This is a special kind of life path, for at times it calls for you to look deep within, and make sense of your emotions and beliefs, and also their source of origin.

Indigo Life paths make excellent psychotherapists, for you are always looking at what is happening behind the scenes and what makes people tick. If someone acts negatively, you will ask yourself what has happened to this person, to make him or her act in this particular way.

Family life is important to you, you like nothing more than having all the family together for holidays and special occasions. Do not forget Indigo people also like solitude, allow yourself this space and time, and importantly allow others this space as well.

At times of stress, you may find yourself becoming more involved with other's problems, rather than dealing with the issue at hand. Try not to allow yourself to become the martyr of the cause and realise people have to experience things for themselves.

Watch out for sight problems and hormonal imbalances at times of great stress.

Live this Indigo life path to its fullest potential and your life will be filled with miracles both big and small, always know they are of your own making. This includes the negative experiences, look upon these as times of learning and times for personal transformation.

Life Path Colour – VIOLET

You have probably found at some time in your life, you have felt different from the rest, let me say that being on a Violet life path it is not surprising. In whatever way you interpreted those feelings; it is positive and all part of being influenced by violet. It makes you stand out from the rest and highlights your natural leadership skills.

When people come to you for advice, they know they will get a sympathetic ear and a true and honest opinion. You have a wonderful gift of being able to synthesise all situations, pull out the positive attributes and come up with a totally new starting point. For those around it may take a while to work out what you've said, reason being the answer seems a little too obvious and they cannot believe the solution was right in front of them all the time.

Violet people have strong beliefs, and when you believe in something, you believe in it with a passion. You would think nothing of making your beliefs known to others, and do not be surprised if you find yourself on some sort of platform, sharing this with others. You can often see what needs to be changed in the world, to make it 'Heaven on Earth' for everyone.

With an eye for beauty, you love to surround yourself with exquisite belongings but see beauty as not merely skin-deep. You have an air of grace and elegance about you, and leave a marked impression long after you have gone. Violet is the colour of opulence, fine art, antiques and design, if you are influenced by this colour, you have a strong need to express these desires. Others may perceive you as being aloof, cold and distant; this is far from the truth.

You have a wild and vivid imagination and often your ideas are ahead of the times, which is why a career in the creative field is important for you, you help the rest of the world move on and change. The world needs violet people to live out their true potential. A career as an actor/actress would appeal; it allows you to safely explore deep emotions through playing characters that share similar emotions to yourself. A poet or writer often expresses himself through his work, yet can still, to some degree remain detached from his feelings.

When stressed, be-aware of not becoming blinked or controlling of others just because they do not share your farsighted plans. Learn to say how you feel and not totally withdraw into yourself.

You are like a delicate flower; one of a kind, with the right kind of love and understanding you will flourish and grow.

Life Path Colour – ROSE

A Rose life path offers you direct contact with spirituality, it also gives you a strong link to an earthly existence, and you can act in either one, and will do so with great achievement in both. You act as guide to those that have lost their way, and will gladly offer comfort and support. Rose is what you might call the administrator; you keep things together and help them run smoothly. You take people's plans and ideas and help them become a reality, being totally selfless by nature you much prefer to take a background role, and let someone else be in the limelight. You expect from others only as much as you are prepared to do for yourself. You will constantly try to help others to express themselves to their fullest potential; you are persistent and will give your all to obtain your goals.

Rose people often move around the world, if you are not off travelling the globe for a year or two, you will find you have direct links with other continents, be it through work or social life. You believe the world and beyond, are ultimately all one force, and try as we might, to think or prove otherwise, we are all indirectly related.

You are friendly and loving to those around you, yet sometimes you forget that you need loving and support as well. This is because you are often so busy playing host to the rest of the world, you ignore things closer to home, and it can lead to feelings of isolation and loneliness.

At times of stress, your tolerance level becomes minimal, and people are most surprised at how you suddenly erupt like a volcano. Physical conditions could manifest as lower back problems and recurring knocks and bruises.

Life Path Colour – GOLD

A Gold life path is one of a natural teacher, whether you teach professionally or not you will often find yourself passing on relevant information. Gold could be described, as much like a library you always know where to go or who to contact, if not a library then likened to a sage. You were born wise, and from an early age people around you would tell of their concerns and worries, you could have felt that at times, like Hercules you too were carrying the world on your shoulders.

You achieve much on your journey through life, and have many talents. It could take many years before you actually recognise your own abilities and gifts, and what you have to offer humanity as a whole. You are a bright light to any dull corner. Gold people usually possess a natural healing ability; this comes about more through your words of wisdom.

Obviously there are two sides to every coin, be-aware of not becoming over critical of others or to authoritarian in your approach. A gold person has to achieve absolute perfection, anything less is considered a failure. You have a powerful inner-critic that constantly reminds you of what you have yet to master, and how you can improve yourself, this inner critic is never satisfied.

You are emotional by nature and need to express the strong feelings, keep them locked up, and you may be setting yourself up for aching joints, low self-esteem, and weakness in the immune system.

Learn to balance your two opposites and you will find a whole New World of childlike fun and laughter opens up for you. Follow this golden rule and you will have discovered your very own elixir of life.

Once you begin to understand your colour needs, you can utilise all the information provided in this booklet. Decorate with the appropriate shades and tints wear the colours you feel drawn towards and colour will do the rest. It will activate the healer within, unlock and help heal past hurts, but above all you will realise the journey across the rainbow is worth its weight in gold.

Colour in all its forms is a vast and varied subject and this is only the tip of the iceberg.

Whisper the language of colour; express the voice of the Universe.

Mark offers the following: -

Private Consultations
Colour Parties
Corporate Events
Retreats
Talks
Workshops

Further information: -

Email: mark@colourforlife.com
Website: www.colourforlife.com

MARK WENTWORTH

Global Colour Ambassador Mark Wentworth has been studying and working with colour for over 30 years. He is the creator of the Colour PsychoDynamic method and Co-creator of Dynamic Theatre, both integrating the archetypal and visionary worlds of Carl Jung. Mark is based in the UK as well as working across eleven countries worldwide. He continues to Add a Little Colour to the lives of many.

Printed in Poland
by Amazon Fulfillment
Poland Sp. z o.o., Wrocław

63123519R00038